The Visible World

The Visible World

Pier Giorgio Di Cicco

Mansfield Press

Printed in Canada

Library and Archives Canada Cataloguing in Publication

Di Cicco, Pier Giorgio, 1949-
The visible world / Pier Giorgio Di Cicco.

Poems.
ISBN 1-894469-26-7

I. Title.

PS8557.248V58 2006 C811'.54 C2006-902245-3

Some of the poems in The Visible World have been published in The Toronto Star and The Catholic Register.

Design: Mansfield Creative
Cover Photo: iStockphoto

The publication of The Visible World has been generously supported by The Canada Council for the Arts and The Ontario Arts Council.

Mansfield Press Inc.
25 Mansfield Avenue, Toronto, Ontario, Canada M6J 2A9
Publisher: Denis De Klerck
www.mansfieldpress.net

The Canada Council for the Arts since 1957 | Le Conseil des Arts du Canada depuis 1957

Ontario Arts Council
Conseil des Arts de l'Ontario

Dedicated to Glen McGuire

Table of Contents

I believe that God is in me
as the sun is in the colour and fragrance
of a flower—
the Light in my darkness,
the Voice in my silence.

Helen Keller

1

The Sound of Shimmer

The Poems the Dead Get

A world of wonder, the sparrows picking
the bread I left in the snowy field; my life,
its episodes, the flowers I bring—
what is left of my eyes.

Under a larch tree,
under that larch tree in the far field this snowy,
sun-filled day, I am making up the figure
of a woman; she is stringing together a rosary
of all those I have ever loved. I will wear it
like an amulet. Not admonishing—
the voices of the dead; just prayerful, urging me
on to the next thing. To try anything, in
faith, in trust.

The Sound of Shimmer

my father's old transistor radio
is itself, a piece of work
of art that is my
heart; it catches bits of
sunlight something like the way
his eyes caught the sun on a day like this.

my mother too is in the white
explosion of the fleshed out sun
of radiance; things like her laundry line,
and eggs frothed in the sunday of all bells.
there are, extraordinary in the movements, uncles,
prayers and violets, highways,
a peck on the cheek.
    there is no reason not to bless and be
blessed for the moment between terror
and ignorance.
that too I offer up.

I give myself to planks and fences
and dead men
I almost saw loving me.

since I am a man who does not have children
I make legitimate sunlight of the helpless
matter of my life,

and I offer not prose, or salt-shakers,
but my inverted, soul and question,
answered in cupped hands and loving—
to see if I would walk into the yard
and be touched, like skin,
for blessing.

About This Life

The words of friends,
so sad,
grey; loved, in spite
of them. Twenty
years gone into
joining mind and body, chopped
by lost affairs, dead dreams.

Friends, asleep with hopes, pains.
Their brains forget,
in a wash of cricket chirps.

The child lives on,
and never returns to certain places.

I watch these words, with bones
so tiny they can't be mended.

Waste

when I think of the years I've wasted
standing on my farm, the
amazing king of waste,
    I know I am made for fodder of the
lunatic stars, am made for dawn to collect,
like a songster turned inwards—what God
can't fathom.

when I am the stars I've wasted, not seen, myself
made carrion for what must be saved,

I rejoice not in the made, but in what must be
undone to save myself,

like judas.

—when I see the song cannot be done until
I exacerbate him, his
impatience trickling like rain, on me, to grow,
what must, behind the armour of my skin,
be golden,

I blush and baulk and fear, and dance like
a two footed man riveted on the planet
like obstinacy, what must be saved,
to make him a consolation.

wasted, and not irremediably,
but wholly; mine and not, for lights to
shine into my eyes to see me light
myself, what must be shone like
giver of the love He is in me,

endowment of what is to grow,
like homonym for man, a pair of starry
eyes, squinting for
plain creation.

Angelie

my cousin angelie who I have never seen
came to my thoughts today.

hello angelina, whom I never saw except for *maybe.*

my life is ruinously ok.
                                        and leaves and brooks,

and sounds that make no sense when people speak them,
and music not my own.
I hope your own
is mended and wherever how, like birds or insects
may these thoughts go find you.

and speaking from behind the bush of
incredulity at who we are, made out from
a bit of clay,
say in Arizona or behind some roadside stand
you pass by on the way to *mottle* or *agree,*
I wave.

I had meant to write, but body like encasement kept me
like a human being, away.

looking forward to the effacement
of the world to greet you.

Screaming at the Pyramids

you can hear the screams
the deft blow
bones for the making.

this is different song.
          mine.
it is being beaten, under the world.
it is brother
cruelty and no brother.

it is not sassafras song,
nor nightingale. it is my sister
fled to the songless.
my bones she wears and the felt
bones of others.
her cries redeem, under juniper and
lamplight, on ocean and dreams.
her wind-wail.

I will not make too much of my sister;
it is brother cruelty I want crucified to
stars and night's opal.
it is my dog-brother I want terrified
in me,
this mystery, iniquitous, let
scamper from the father's hand,
like forced creation.

Doing Funerals

There are the wailers,
the black harridans,
the faith-filled.
I buried the babies. I buried the man
who bought me the suit
I wore when I buried him.

Death has no feelings for me.
Death is rich. I plant it.
The harvest is other.

I am the song.
The live blessing,
the lily
in the flesh.

The First Immigrants

They die, like rain.

I tried to take care of them,
like prose; that is a lie. They fell
        from my fingers;
not even like snow, they died.
Like rain.

Images of tenderness
they left me—
a lock of hair,
a new breath,
the poetry that is like
what I dry my tears with,
a recognition of art like
what I try to restore as
two halves of a heart
poised above the waters of
love.

A sentiment is what
I bury them with; the shawl
of the family.

I give them all the excesses
they pined for: a country,
8mm films come to life,
images of a language,
a boy in my head, writing for them,
that they may walk out of the grave.

I leave them to God, foremostly,
who by the hand ushered them, and
shone in the eyes like a hope,
a sunny day,
in the garden of their dreams
in a backyard off College Street.
I too would have liked a garden like that,
to keep forever.

Like my eyes, now I give them
my salutation of six feet and much,
papers and photographs,
like an earth's centre,
whom I have buried, like myself,
grown out of them.

Then

sometime I think I have
    no more

tears in me, basically,
and no more voice, except
    for guts
and a little bit of
    dead silence called "ma,"
and that little bit of
star fodder I use for brains, and the toes
of God that are my grave, and the news of
me gurgling down the planet like
children with their hair on fire.

innocence, my repose in

twenty thousand years, and sharp
images, damn them, that are my candy cane
and sugared.

and love that is my demise and
rhetoric of would have,
and for you, on first meeting,
a face, full of need and
    ballast of every-which thing, wanted,
spoiled like cream, and then,
a sunset.

and this is how like this, we come together,
humans, gnarled, like wood
perhaps, and grief,

or just sandboxed, like an ocean
without children.
me, my hand, your heart, your brain and
whatever's left over, like a blown kiss
from God.

Burying

it's a nightmare. they go faster than I
can bless, or venerate them;
in they go... into the crypt—
the funeral director says the family
didn't want closure, didn't wait to see
their dead sealed into the wall.

didn't want to see grandma forklifted into
a mausoleum wall. ontario. they wrap up the dead
to keep the microbes in.

I held my mother's body in my arms.
then I put her in the body-bag;
you gotta be fast.

nothing to do with the fake or the living, this business
of death. God is reeling them in faster and faster.

I drive in the hearse; looking; macdonald's, pneumatic drills, curses
in traffic; I go by in the hearse and I wonder
if the wakeful will let us be
when we want to sleep.

thank God the spirit goes elsewise we cannot imagine,
I wouldn't want to be so close

to the antiseptic and the noisy;
and the dead won't need me and my
brain and heart that wants to give them an emotion
like a feather.
God understands the needs of the living.

it is need at the foot of the coffin, it is the incense rising
like a prayer wafting the dead as if they weren't going
up on their own steam, or reeled in, faster than
I can say a prayer, or anything. it's the
fishing that God does, faster than I

can pray.
it is my understanding that breaks like a back,
like the death I am preparing for.

The Pastor of Them

I gave them sock and dew,
wind and blood, blessing and
restitution; they gave me absence like the
wind I was the sail of.

I came home to myself to find them—
what angels thanked me of,
and loneliness like hands that
looked for me.

I am now what needs to
bless them, like a body without
speech.

leaves, I might have been. dead leaves.
or rain cloud before sun,
or just their baptized child with a hat
of noon, and laughter that
dishevels winter eves.

what I miss of them in me,
is service, like what I am
sprouted from the planet to
make light a stitching for
more light.

happier in their homes,
I am what is husked, like what was
harvested to make them awake.

much of what I am is
their betrothal to what came of them,
from the creator's mouth.

Love

I endure God,
my hunger and cruelty.

beyond that murky hill where God
will not show his face, I look with eyes
that endure, on the innocent fall of
butterflies.

I see all and anything
in faith, and nothing more.

Night, the Visits

If our self-reliance could be crushed by some gentler means, would not the Beloved have found it? – JOHN BENTLEY-MAYS

and then also, I found a bat on the road,
dead, and another one last year, satiated on the
grease in the sink.
killed another, and stopped, caught the rest in butterfly nets.
went blind to hear Him coming from me like my moth to light;
everywhere, I have spent and killed myself, and cherished
myself like a dead thing, killed of His mercy and
reawakened.

am I an angel, or a deaf thing with eyes,
that he must scatter like a hope in me, like light
I wish for? if I could see
truly, what my existence is a glove for.

a thing, a bird, a moth, a bat falls on my
window screen at night. I do not know which it is,
like my own heart beating to get out.
so softly and much more gentle
are my eyelids
like His love for me
that I will open to the dawn,
to find Him.

Landowner

The wilderness is the nightmare
you wake from;
you check the cupboards,
go to the window and
and return to your conscience.
The nightmare is the man you were,
laughing
for the goodness betrothed.
The wilderness tolls at any hour
as the riders of judgement pass.

You move from the window
with a stone face.

The sun rises
between the portals of
what might have been, given
one more drop of blood.

And the shy animals come to the gate
and stand at the garden and the stream,
innocent of the hand that feeds them.

Illumination

steam too rising from the pot on the stove. a clock
that is two hours behind.
clumps of snow on what is left of
last year's mountain ash; the berries sullen,
not bright red as they were in summer.
a ghost walks through
the trees, handing me my life.
and the peels of laughter rise from the loved or dead.
so little to make a clearing for.
I will jump in with my tears perhaps, shed skin,
let the brightness of a piece of glass
catch light. it is all
I know of ideas—the hard world living outside of us;
behind which I have lived my life
suckling for love, for God, the impresario, his
confabulations, made nothing of, outside the
strainer that I am.
I am so happy.
it is a lie, lousy as I am with bricks and mortar, and wood
and whatever things are made of, excellent things,
outside my hungering heart.

Alba

The new dawn again
anoints itself, this many seasons after,
coming like its brothers, that woke my dreams;
settles in the sunny, augers me,
this music of myself, cowled in God,
on a trunk of wood, on any morning star.

Happy with it, forgetting the rapes,
and hee-haws, blundering nights.
What is this hurrier,
steady towards me, promising.
Destructive be-all.
I am not for it. Dissolution is
here, in what I swatched back to God;
for not on time, His being.
Too late this dawn, audit of, what could have been,
in my mouth now, like a rind, like a letter to
the long lost
dead.

In Search Of

my mother is buried
so many miles away in my heart;
if I could unbury her, bring back—
forgotten rigamaroles,
slanting kisses, moons of sun and sun
in moons. oh, if I, so much, could bring back,

like
the sleep of a child, and those things, all,
I nuzzled closely to, my branches, bare,
of grazing hopes, my yesterday.

if I, unlike my mother, were not so
many miles from everything
I have loved,

a letter I would write
to the animal that is my heart.

My Father's Ring

my father's ring is
white and pale, no, black and
golden, fits me like a body
green with spring, is
like my mind, adult,
and simple like his hand with
his ring on it.

though I never wear it,
I see it
caressing my face,

running down the keys
of an accordion.

I wear it and am afraid, I might become what he had
meant to walk the earth as—
hope and flowerlets.

it must be worn and isn't.

it is what drops from heaven
or grows from the earth like
an empire of grace.

it is opal. did I tell you?
my father's conscience on me—

then again (let's finish this) is
what I would have made of breath
like the moth stunted on the summer screen—

his voice trying to come into me
to finish gentleness
and dream
a son,

that I will fit that ring,
like clouds around my
neck,
like dew or rain
become of him.

Metamorphosis

What doesn’t change
is what you will become.

Be still and let things draw themselves
to you
as you draw near.

You are changed by
the syllables of creation.

Your business is the metaphor you are.
You are the fountain, brimming, cresting away;

are you the mist,
or the blue that reaches like a bough of water?

You are the breath of air
that one day wafts the morning lily,
and soon will drift from tree to tree
in autumn's reach.

Your tears are what is
human, pausing to take a breath in
the timeless
and its yearning for you;

you are the face of creation,
turning to the new light—

the light that you call dawn,
when night was never yours.

What change?
You have become yourself.

How Not to Believe in the World

look at all the people that
will sing to you only in your sleep

who need you only when you're down and
out, the heroism that is behind
cannisters and brooks,
the moonlight wasted, the coughing spell
that spells "who for."

I am behind the mean and miserable,
the voice of love that says come to me (you did
not, last time), but I have waited, looking
like heart and diamond, grist and grief.

I am the only valentine you will ever have,
everywhere, the littlest thing that you are
grateful for, the bits of universe demanding
hope from you and dishing back
a reason for your staying alive.

I am love, your eyes, the sentiment that returns
before spring, the belief in yourself that was just
an excuse for lilacs. I am everywhere and nowhere,
neither obvious nor special. I dress in no person,
but I hear your voice in every word, saying paradise.

My Father's Love

I found my dad's transistor radio,
in the country dark.
I too will die. I am close to my father.
Fireflies and things
bring him to me.

Almost I can touch him, say goodbye to
things without malice, just
roses and things he had given.

I think I will see him. Our love is
that strong.

I hope we enjoy what we did not, my father
and I. His hand reached out and gave me the
transistor radio. What else would he not
give me? From that little star, furniture,
record albums, days of sun and rain
spill out.

Such a tiny window to enter through.
Such small hands.

II

Forgiveness in the Dark

Songsters

here I am singing writing as you
bequeath, behest, demand with teeth
like dandelions, up the side of brook and
wall and tears and laugh
down the trickle of my inside that is
name, like me, of dust.

is it the coyote
is it faith or chance,
is it my arm made of blood or just pining
and wishing that makes me lean towards you
like planet for the moon, like this and that,
like rhetoric, like plush fruit for
maw of inarticulate man?

I love you like myself,
I will go small like a grief
unto mine eyes that your hands are.

singing and writing and dancing into the grave
that is beauty and music.

cavern and marmoset have your spelling too,
whom I will whisper to. we are strings and violin
for what won't play out in the stars; man and
meditating things, blood and arc of
love.

Prayer of Finding

Here I will find Him,
in an alphabet of loon and otter.

And the impulse to go to mother
will be laid to rest like a child.

There is no need,
and I will respect the helping hand
when I am found.
But I will search nothing.

I am like a stone. I wait,
and dream of sunlight.

If only these arteries looked like
stone. They scream flowers
where the body has not forsaken me.

There is something I have not understood about
these arteries; how they are like waters in a canyon
carving out stone to make it look beautiful.

Blood, then, is for carving.
I am not stone. I am sleeping artisan.

I cannot carve myself into masterpiece,
but by the waters through somebody else's life,
I make a beautiful thought of fields and otter.
I am the poem my throat cannot make.

And my throat is not stone;
it is what sings like rain, as I have waited,

and the sunlight has arrived, by something other than me,
and I am, like the loon and otter,

alphabet, and found.

Alluding to Song

there is a kind of poem that God listens to; it has
to do with hunger, or the secret of the day,
a fly on a pane, yesterday's rabbit tracks.
the poem refused that may get used
not knowing
what will come of it,

the stone rejected,
the song He won't call song,
but a hand
unconscious of its need.

we are not fed by the right hand.
and the poem without this arrogance
is the first phonetic
of star-gazing. the constellations do not
ask why we should love so much in a
an orbit of skin and bones.

It is wonder—

this call
to be with Him,
like
stardust or woodscape,
where the otter feeds, and calls its
brothers, the
marmoset and sage.

That I Begin

there may be music that comes in,
and sifts the grass, like my hair,
so needing of the saviour's hand.

then too the weather may,
and songs restore me, badgers,
trips; but isolately,
my soul lingers for God.

I am not gathering today, but picking
what is left.
I plant a kiss
on memory, with the music mostly gone.

I tack photographs onto trees and walls,
and pray
for those who had simple voices,
who are far from me,

as I inch my way through grass,
to a kind of sky, and
imagine.

God Is Like Your Eyes

God is like your eyes.
that is all that can be said
of this summer;
bees, leaves and planes
checker the sky,
mosy along my life,
weaving
like thread,
suturing a torso,
a stumped man for the earth;

I won't return to this.

I found God in the house too.
as a yellow moth.
I thought it was a paper moth—
it kept so still. I thought it had been
there for a long time.
I did not know.

my God
leaves the room,
wistful about the day.

I want to have live, that
which has been without me,

and be weighed down with leaves and bees
and the sight of Him.

A Few Noticeable Things

Susan gave me flowers
        they are perched on the sill.
and the snow concocts its panorama
and there are a few more objects I
love, let's say the shadow of the stems of
the flowers against the wall. there are also fake
flowers in the corner.
I have left the kitchen table lamp on, a small 25 watt bulb
I keep on all the time. kitchen light and sunlight
will marry and have children and be like a custodian to me.

my mother's eyes also come to me as wish
to be complete; the threads of my life woven badly.
should I forgive, or is it done for me?

here is a man of passion then, with the items that
speak to him, saying "speak us"; and that is all passion is;
the muteness, apparently, finding tongue in what can sing
like a type of angel; as things have been rehearsing me
all day long, the live-long day, things
wait to hold me, my song.

I wonder what, in stillness, they do, the world things,
blessed, in languages too subtle for me to hear
past my emotions. but my emotions are what they do not mind
when they ride the crest of them, as if they were going somewhere—
blessed things, by my breath.

and now they tone down by dusk as I reach
out to them. they want to go to another place, a register
of blessing I don't know,
and I look to the aureate snow to go on singing.

but there is a kind of song I must be
slow by, like the place of death that is not death,
the not understood melody I am not from, but must
be music of.

perhaps I will bring my songster ways
to the tenebrous, and will be a new kind of flower
for dying. and that is all "perfecting" is, in song;
to give the earth new resonance by being a lyric
man beneath it.

and so I sing these things by sunlight;
flowers, case, stems and table lamp, as the dusk fades them into
what I cannot speak, unless I become subtle,
like humility, to shine like anything by light
and tone myself down to the created, dark for my ignorance,
but bright every morning thrust that invents what is seen,
irrevocably.

Bring On the Autumn

Why don't you bring the autumn on?

What have I to say to you?
I've no expletives.
I've no joy.

Birds and chipmunks play outside,
they don't move me with your diminutives.

Alvin has his window in the bark,
I've run over Barbara the skunk.
Harvey the garter snake has slunk back out—
a bat charges at me in the dark,

he has your ears and mouth.
God is like a bat, that's funny.
My osteo is breaking my joints,
gravity pulls my jowls down.

I have no mercy in me when I don't feel yours.
and I have bad memory.

I almost remembered on Tuesday
that you saved my life in 1983.
What do I want?

I love wood. It wants nothing, absorbs the residue of
loving tenants and passes it on.
I rub my cheek against the door-posts of my house,
and am loved by wood.
and this is my desert, to be loved by little, and less,

until I am nothing but love.

Silhouettes

Muriel phones to tell me
trees are beautiful without leaves
too

I feel that way

and before long I'll be the tree
she told me to look at—she sees it with leaves,
but Muriel likes to see the good in everything.

maybe this explains
the sadness of this time of year.

she says, look for the silhouette, when the sun goes
down or up,

(as if I knew what time of day it was).
I figure the root and trunk must still be strong
to sprout leaves again next year.

I confess my strength.

Muriel tells me things as I need to
hear them... memories coming out of the brush and forest,
and the animals bring them;

and when I have nothing, these words, these
leaves will come
indifferently.

But My Spirit

The wind, the stars. I raise my
hand to the cloisters of air.
They will remember me as a gesture,
a tiny part of the soul.

When I was young, I never finished poems.
I was well off with
the wind, the unfinished moon,

this scooped out ghost of a brother
whom I kiss,
now and then.

Looking at my Death

where have you gone?
where have I gone?

I have not been myself,
living in fear. I do not
want to be buried next to anyone.

my blades of grass
do not accept your lonely cricket.

What then is Grace

what then is grace, but the uninvented,
that does not come like flowers,

but like breath out of the heart, the mouth, the memory
of God when all that was given is ours.

what then becomes passionate and clear?

that heaven is
will and dreams, gazebos and
coffees,
some vision of singing the mundane,

some furniture
for clouds.

some seduction of
what is beautiful.

I Love This Too

I love this too, the world,
as it comes for me, and in me
and all its paraphernalia which sounds
like the capitol of it.

I have watched dogs have at me
and God shield me,
and thistles too by the side of the road
have sung their alarms at me,
or whatever they were glistening, and

I miss too the world I did not
make much of.
and soil,
and darts.

I am alone now, with big electric
lights on country roads,
and ghosts; dead relatives of my spleen,
whoosh by. How do I talk fast
enough to explain anything?

I say hands, long eyelashes, a book
I did not read.
Watch how my lips flap
in defiance of the stars.

Look how the sky let's drop one
wide tear the size of a city-scape.

What do I want to say that is not
"love me, and want me, oh wood,
with me as your brethren against fencepost
and starlight?"

Sign

God like a moth,
like a baby shrine plastered on
the wall,
or like a triangle with its legs
not stirring.
just a little to remind you
you are on the way home,
blind, like a moth to light,
blind but to heat, blind but to
the electric air.

I must not scare off these living things
that give directions.
I must be careful with sun, moon, stars.

I look at things closely. it is not wonder.
it is stories I hear of chance meetings, murders
and songs.

a long lost uncle is what I need,
but I will not take my eyes off the moth,
in mid-summer, and I will pray for
the lingerers of fall, and I am humble for
winter moths to come.
I am quiet and I wait.
for moths too must become
angels, transform, as I will,
into something with clear eyes,
that can see home.

Driving Dark Roads

I love
that little trailer in the field,
and lights,
and rhythms and
coyotes.

I always
arrive at this trailer in the woods,
to make a butterfly of memories,
on the earth

I watch with autumn eyes
the transcendental leaf,

and the anointed planet.
and I will bless
a man of passion,

this gossamer and wing,
this town I come upon, this place,
myself.

The Wilderness

the wilderness is about
making somebody happy
over and over again,
is about good over evil
and so many other clichés;
it is about more than intelligence—
it is about the softest things having sway
over your life. is about moths and cats
and badgers, closing the door on no one.
it is about marrying yourself—

it is about rising above
any number of things, looking at yourself from above,
the landscapes of you, the mean trajectories,
the bumbling desires going door to door,
rising above and looking down and exonerating.

the greatest things—let's have an understanding—
are not confusing sensuality with passion,
of love with fulfilment,
of heaven with possibility; the greatest things
are about belonging to what you have no command over—
sunsets, tears, and the face that is dearest;
love is about being killed when you lack the inclination—

also;
moths, moths, moths, moths
and the fire, the fire is not hot, the fire is the beloved,
the fire is the legacy, from "legare"—
what ties the fabric of things together, human beings,
what you see between them, that makes
them sense to each other.

the wilderness is knowing this, with or without company.
the wilderness is the embers after the fire,
is nostalgia for what you have given, and grace before
what feeds you next; and the awful patience before God.

Jazz Upper

Beaten into carefree,
beaten careless, that's what we are
by leaf and badger forsaken, much
less by the human.

I have been dancing alone
in my room
for the god, Harvey.

In many places, shoal and
daffodil roof

you have not seen me.

So much of what I am
escaped, dungeon wise
into morning.

A god's periwinkle I am.
I have known shoes, shadow-worn.
I am thinking now of bark,
dusk-taken, and places of urchin dark,
oh maybe upstate New York in
coriander month, homes not invited
into, left eating mandrogola outside,

or just left at a harbour dock.
I am singing, Americas, this new music,

beaten into carefree, beaten into careless,
planet-wise at sunset.

February

the sun is astonishing, barrels
through snow drifts, birch trees,
in hopeful fifties light;

white caterpillars;
I have spent half my life thinking
up descriptions of snow,

and I am left with that—
the
delicate carnations on the window ledge.

and orange light,
brown branches,
bottles,
and blessed things.

Forgiveness in the Dark

grace arrives; the body
hears. tears bless. blood is
unlocked from the heart.

this then, the gifts of love.

savaged by their hurts and needs,
my friends
do nothing for anyone but themselves.

I love them with stars, and poetry, and nights.
and sacred words,

and watch God lose a day and lose nothing.

PIER GIORGIO DI CICCO was born in Arezzo, Italy and was raised in Montreal, Toronto and Baltimore. He is a Roman Catholic Priest, Curator of the Toronto Humanitas Project and teaches at the University of Toronto. He writes for The Toronto Star and consults on issues of global aesthetic.

ALSO BY PIER GIORGIO DI CICCO

We Are the Light Turning (1975, revised 1976)
The Sad Facts (1977)
The Circular Dark (1977)
Dancing in the House of Cards (1977)
A Burning Patience (1978)
Dolce-Amaro (1978)
The Tough Romance (1979, 1990)
translated as *Les Amour Difficiles* (1990)
A Straw Hat for Everything (1981)
Flying Deeper into the Century (1982)
Dark to Light: Reasons for Humanness, Poems 1976 – 1979 (1983)
Women We Never See Again (1984)
Post-Sixties Nocturne (1985)
Virgin Science: Hunting Holistic Paradigms (1986)
Living in Paradise—New and Selected Poems (2001)
The Honeymoon Wilderness (2002)
The Dark Time of Angels (2003)
Dead Men of the Fifties (2004)

AS EDITOR
Roman Candles: An Anthology of Seventeen Italo-Canadian Poets (1978)